TEAM SPIRIT ®

SMART BOOKS FOR YOUNG FANS

THE TEXAS RANGERS

BY

MARK STEWART

NORWOOD HOUSE 🏠 PRESS

CHICAGO, ILLINOIS

Norwood House Press
P.O. Box 316598
Chicago, Illinois 60631

For information regarding Norwood House Press, please visit our website at:
www.norwoodhousepress.com or call 866-565-2900.

All photos courtesy of Getty Images except the following:
Tom DiPace (4, 9, 10, 11, 14, 17, 25, 38),
Topps, Inc. (6, 7, 19, 20, 21, 26, 27, 28, 35 top left & right, 42 bottom, 45), SSPC (15),
SportsChrome (18, 36, 41), A.M. Briggs & Co. (30), Washington Senators (33),
TCMA, Ltd. (34 top), Author's Collection (34 bottom),
Black Book Partners Archives (40, 42 top, 43 left), Matt Richman (48).
Cover Photo: Ezra Shaw/Getty Images

The memorabilia and artifacts pictured in this book are presented for educational and informational purposes,
and come from the collection of the author.

Editor: Mike Kennedy
Designer: Ron Jaffe
Project Management: Black Book Partners, LLC.
Special thanks to Topps, Inc.

Library of Congress Cataloging-in-Publication Data

Stewart, Mark, 1960-
  The Texas Rangers / by Mark Stewart. -- Library ed.
      p. cm. -- (Team spirit)
  Includes bibliographical references and index.
  Summary: "A Team Spirit Baseball edition featuring the Texas Rangers that
chronicles the history and accomplishments of the team. Includes access to
the Team Spirit website, which provides additional information, updates and
photos"--Provided by publisher.
  ISBN 978-1-59953-499-2 (library : alk. paper) -- ISBN 978-1-60357-379-5
(ebook) 1. Texas Rangers (Baseball team)--History--Juvenile literature.
I. Title.
  GV875.T4S84 2012mi
  796.357'6409764531--dc23
                                          2011048459

Manufactured in the United States of America in North Mankato, Minnesota.
196N—012012

COVER PHOTO: The Rangers celebrate a win during the 2011 season.

TABLE OF CONTENTS

ABOUT OUR GLOSSARY

In this book, there may be several words that you are reading for the first time. Some are sports words, some are new vocabulary words, and some are familiar words that are used in an unusual way. All of these words are defined on page 46. Throughout the book, sports words appear in **bold type**. Regular vocabulary words appear in ***bold italic type***.

MEET THE RANGERS

Baseball players are taught to be patient. The greater the pressure they face, the more they must relax and trust that their talent will shine through. The same could be said for fans of the Texas Rangers. They went almost 40 years before their team made it to the **World Series**.

How did the Rangers reward the patience of their fans? The team found just the right mix of pitching and hitting, and the wins started coming easily. For many years, the Rangers had fallen short of a league championship. That is no longer true—today Texas can proudly say it has won a **pennant**.

This book tells the story of the Rangers. They began in another part of the country in the 1960s and moved west in the 1970s. It may have taken them a while to get used to their new address, but these days the Rangers are feeling right at home in Texas.

Nelson Cruz returns to the dugout after scoring another run for the power-packed Rangers.

5

GLORY DAYS

The Rangers are one of two teams that were once called the Washington Senators. (The other is the Minnesota Twins.) In 1961, the Senators moved to Minnesota after 60 seasons in Washington, D.C. A new team—also called the Senators—replaced

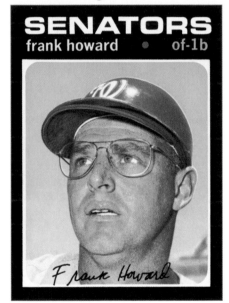

them in the nation's capital. Baseball fans who cheered for the Senators in 1960 rooted for an entirely different group of Senators in 1961!

The new Senators played in the **American League (AL)**. They were made up of unwanted players from other clubs. The team found a few diamonds in the rough, including pitchers Claude Osteen and Ron Kline, plus hitters Chuck Hinton and Don Lock. A trade with the Los Angeles Dodgers in 1964 brought Frank Howard to the Senators. He became one of the most feared sluggers in baseball.

LEFT: Frank Howard hit more than 40 homers three years in a row for the Senators.
RIGHT: Third baseman Buddy Bell was known for his glove as well as his bat.

The team's first winning season came in 1969. The Senators hired former **All-Star** Ted Williams to be their manager. Williams was a great student—and teacher—of hitting. The team's batting average soared, and Washington raised its record to 86–76. Unfortunately, the Senators did not keep improving. Soon they were looking for a new home.

In 1972, the team moved from Washington to Arlington, Texas and became the Rangers. Since the club did not have a lot of great hitters, it focused on pitching. During the next *decade*, the Rangers had some of the best pitchers in baseball, including Fergie Jenkins, Gaylord Perry, Jim Bibby, Bert Blyleven, Doc Medich, Jon Matlack, and Charlie Hough.

By the late 1970s, the Rangers were also a good team at the plate. Their offense was led by Buddy Bell, Al Oliver, Mike Hargrove, Toby Harrah, and Richie Zisk. In the 1980s, more talented hitters

joined the team. Larry Parrish, Pete O'Brien, Gary Ward, Ruben Sierra, and Pete Incaviglia gave Texas fans something to cheer about as the team tried to reach the **playoffs** for the first time.

Finally, in the 1990s, the Rangers became true pennant *contenders*. The team's top two stars were Ivan Rodriguez and Juan Gonzalez. Rodriguez was the league's best catcher, and Gonzalez was a dangerous slugger who was named the AL **Most Valuable Player (MVP)** twice. The pair was surrounded by smart, hardworking teammates such as Will Clark, Rusty Greer, and Mark McLemore.

The Rangers made it to the playoffs in 1996, 1998, and 1999. Each time, they lost to the New York Yankees. The Rangers had plenty of hitters, but they lacked the pitching needed to reach the World Series.

LEFT: Fans and teammates called Ivan Rodriguez "Pudge." His nickname can be seen on his chest protector. **ABOVE**: Juan Gonzalez was nicknamed "Juan Gone" for his long home runs.

In the years that followed, Texas tried to overpower opponents with even more offense. The Rangers added sluggers such as Alex Rodriguez, Alfonso Soriano, Hank Blalock, and Mark Teixeira. By then, the team was playing in a fantastic new stadium that hitters loved. But Texas struggled to keep opponents from scoring runs. Finally, the team decided to get serious about pitching. Texas began signing young pitchers out of high school and college. The Rangers also traded for pitchers they thought would get better with more coaching.

Texas made another smart move when it brought back Nolan Ryan to run the team. Ryan had been a great pitcher for the Rangers in the 1990s. As team president, and later owner, Ryan helped put together a very good pitching staff. It included C.J. Wilson, Colby Lewis, Derek Holland, Matt Harrison, Scott Feldman, Alexei Ogando, and Neftali Feliz. Many baseball fans hadn't heard much about these pitchers, but they soon found out who they were.

In 2010 and 2011, the Rangers combined these pitchers with a powerful lineup that included All-Stars Michael Young, Nelson Cruz, Ian Kinsler, and Josh Hamilton. The result was two **AL West** crowns, two AL pennants, and two trips to the World Series. Now that they know the winning formula, the Rangers and their fans expect to be championship contenders every season.

LEFT: Mark Teixeira specialized in driving in runs.
ABOVE: Josh Hamilton hit 57 homers for Texas in 2010 and 2011.

HOME TURF

In their first year as the Senators, the team played in Griffith Stadium in the nation's capital. For the rest of their time in Washington, the Senators played in D.C. Stadium. It was renamed Robert F. Kennedy Memorial Stadium in 1968. The first home of the Rangers after moving to Texas was Arlington Stadium. It was built into the ground, so fans would enter from the top of the stadium and walk down to their seats.

In 1994, the team moved to a new ballpark. It combines an old-time feel with many modern features. The stadium is totally enclosed except for a narrow space in right field. It would take a perfect hit, but one day someone may launch a home run that completely leaves the stadium.

BY THE NUMBERS

- The Rangers' stadium has 49,170 seats.
- The distance from home plate to the left field foul pole is 332 feet.
- The distance from home plate to the center field fence is 400 feet.
- The distance from home plate to the right field foul pole is 325 feet.

This view of the Rangers' stadium shows the narrow space through which a home run would have to travel to leave the ballpark.

DRESSED FOR SUCCESS

T he 1960 Senators and 1961 Senators were completely different teams, yet they looked very similar on the field. Both teams wore white uniforms with blue and red trim. The first big change to that style came in 1968, when red became the team's main color.

After the club moved to Texas, the players went back to wearing red, white, and blue. The letter *T* replaced the letter *W* on their caps. The team's **logo** was the state of Texas with the initials *TR* on it. Today, the logo features a baseball with a big red *T* on it.

Jeff Burroughs   OF   Texas Rangers

By the 1990s, the Rangers had changed their uniform to look more like it did in the 1960s. First they used the mostly blue style and then the mostly red style. Today, the Rangers sometimes wear uniforms with an all-red jersey or an all-blue jersey.

LEFT: Elvis Andrus wears the team's 2011 road uniform.
ABOVE: Jeff Burroughs wears a 1970s road uniform. The *T* on the team's cap has changed little over the years.

WE WON!

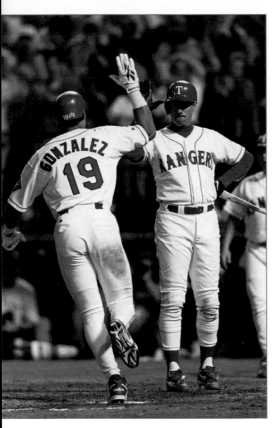

During the 1990s, Texas fans were sure that the Rangers would soon reach their first World Series. The team finished first in the AL West four times from 1994 to 1999. However, despite the power hitting of players such as Juan Gonzalez, Ivan Rodriguez, Will Clark, and Rafael Palmeiro, the Rangers were unable to win a pennant. More than a decade passed before Texas had the talent to make another run at the World Series

The Rangers had a long time to think about their playoff losses. In 2008, the team hired Nolan Ryan as team president. Later he became part-owner of the club. Ryan's job was to run the business off the field, but he also spent plenty of time with the team's young pitchers. He told them not to be afraid of hitters. They had to trust their talent and dare opponents to swing at their best pitches.

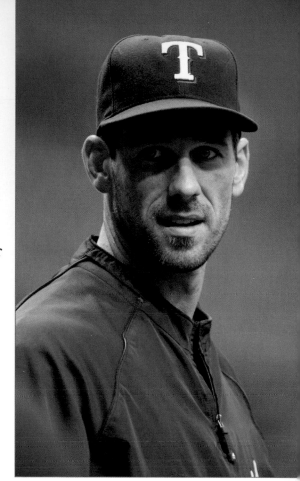

LEFT: Will Clark congratulates Juan Gonzalez after a home run during the 1998 playoffs.
RIGHT: The trade for Cliff Lee in 2010 gave the Rangers a much-needed ace.

The Rangers got the message. In 2010, they won the AL West for the first time since 1999. Texas led the league in hits and batting average. Josh Hamilton was one of four Rangers to smash 20 or more home runs. He was named league MVP. But it was pitching that made the difference for the Rangers. They gave up very few runs and struck out a lot of batters.

That July, Texas improved its pitching even more by trading for Cliff Lee. He instantly became the team's ace. The Rangers cruised into the playoffs and defeated the Tampa Bay Rays in the first round. Lee was sensational. He faced David Price twice and beat him both times. The Rays scored only 13 runs in five games.

Next, the Rangers faced the New York Yankees in the **American League Championship Series (ALCS)**. The teams had met in the playoffs three times during the 1990s, and the Yankees won each time. In the opening game, Texas blew a 5–1 lead and lost. Rangers' fans were afraid that 2010 would be just like all those other years.

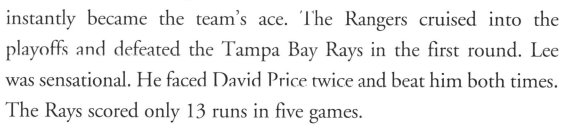

Texas quickly turned things around. The pitching staff allowed just five runs over the next three games. Lee threw another gem in Game 3, beating the Yankees 8–0. The Rangers went on to win the ALCS in six games. It was sweet revenge for Rangers fans. More important, at long last the team had its first pennant!

Unfortunately, the Rangers fell to the red-hot San Francisco Giants in the 2010 World Series. But as soon as the final out was made, Ryan and manager Ron Washington began planning for 2011. They added sluggers Adrian Beltre and Mike Napoli to improve the offense. Cliff Lee left the team as a **free agent**, so the Rangers asked young Derek Holland to fill his shoes. Holland took advantage of the opportunity. He won 16 games for Texas and led the AL with four **shutouts**.

The Rangers won the AL West again. In the playoffs, they defeated the Rays in a rematch of their 2010 series. Beltre was the hitting star. In Game 4, he smashed three home runs.

DEREK HOLLAND
Pitcher

Texas Rangers®

The Rangers next faced the Detroit Tigers in the ALCS. The series was very close until Game 6. With a chance to return to the World Series, the Texas bats exploded for a 15–5 victory. Nobody did more damage than Nelson Cruz. In the six games, he smashed six homers and drove in 13 runs. Cruz was named the series MVP.

After 39 seasons without a pennant, the Rangers now had won two in a row. They seemed ready to win their first World Series. Texas faced the St. Louis Cardinals and won three of the first five games. Holland, C.J. Wilson, and Colby Lewis all threw great games.

The Rangers were one strike away from a championship in Game 6 when disaster struck. The Cardinals tied the game and went on to win in extra innings. In Game 7, the **bullpen**—which had been so good all year long—failed. The Rangers watched in frustration as the Cardinals won 6–2. It was an exciting series that reminded Texas baseball fans just how hard it is to reach the top of the sport.

ABOVE: Nolan Ryan sits in the Texas dugout during the 2010 World Series. He was already thinking about how to improve the team for 2011.
RIGHT: Derek Holland

GO-TO GUYS

To be a true star in baseball, you need more than a quick bat and a strong arm. You have to be a "go-to guy"—someone the manager wants on the pitcher's mound or in the batter's box when it matters most. Fans of the Senators and Rangers have had a lot to cheer about over the years, including these great stars …

THE PIONEERS

FRANK HOWARD   Outfielder/First Baseman

• BORN: 8/8/1936   • PLAYED FOR TEAM: 1965 TO 1972

Frank Howard was a huge man who looked like he could have played basketball. Not surprisingly, he hit the ball very hard and very far. Howard led the AL in home runs twice and **runs batted in (RBIs)** once.

TOBY HARRAH   Shortstop/
                                   Third Baseman

• BORN: 10/26/1948

• PLAYED FOR TEAM: 1969 TO 1978 & 1985 TO 1986

Toby Harrah was a very patient hitter. When he did see a pitch he liked, he often hit it a long way. Few shortstops in the 1970s could match Harrah's power.

AL OLIVER Outfielder

- BORN: 10/14/1946   • PLAYED FOR TEAM: 1978 TO 1981

Al Oliver played four seasons in Texas. He batted better than .300 each year and set a personal high with 117 RBIs in 1980. He was an All-Star three times for the Rangers.

CHARLIE HOUGH Pitcher

- BORN: 1/5/1948   • PLAYED FOR TEAM: 1980 TO 1990

Charlie Hough had a great **knuckleball**, and he used it to win 139 games for the Rangers. He was always among the AL leaders in **complete games** and innings pitched.

RUBEN SIERRA Outfielder

- BORN: 10/6/1965   • PLAYED FOR TEAM: 1986 TO 1992, 2000 TO 2001 & 2003

Baseball came easily to Ruben Sierra. Within a few years of joining the Rangers at the age of 20, he led the AL in RBIs. Sierra hit with power from both sides of the plate and had a cannon for an arm.

NOLAN RYAN Pitcher

- BORN: 1/31/1947   • PLAYED FOR TEAM: 1989 TO 1993

Nolan Ryan was 42 years old when he joined the Rangers. Some wondered whether the hard-throwing pitcher could still get the job done. Ryan answered his critics by striking out 301 batters in his first season in Texas and pitching **no-hitters** in each of the next two seasons.

LEFT: Toby Harrah
ABOVE: Al Oliver

RAFAEL PALMEIRO   First Baseman/Designated Hitter

- BORN: 9/24/1964
- PLAYED FOR TEAM: 1989 TO 1993 & 1999 TO 2003

Rafael Palmeiro used his smooth swing to become one of baseball's finest hitters. He was also a very good defensive first baseman. Palmeiro led the AL in hits in 1990 and doubles in 1991.

JUAN GONZALEZ   Outfielder

- BORN: 10/20/1969
- PLAYED FOR TEAM: 1989 TO 1999 & 2002 TO 2003

Juan Gonzalez was one of baseball's best power hitters. With Texas, he led the league in home runs twice and drove in more than 100 runs seven times. Gonzalez was the AL MVP in 1996 and 1998.

IVAN RODRIGUEZ   Catcher

- BORN: 11/27/1971   • PLAYED FOR TEAM: 1991 TO 2002

No catcher combined defense, hitting, and speed the way Ivan Rodriguez did. Pudge came to the Rangers at the age of 19 and earned his first **Gold Glove** a year later. He won 10 in all with Texas and was the league MVP in 1999.

MICHAEL YOUNG   Shortstop/Second Baseman

- BORN: 10/19/1976
- FIRST YEAR WITH TEAM: 2000

Michael Young never cared where he played in the field as long as his name was in the starting lineup. He led the league in hits twice, in 2005 and again in 2011. He was an All-Star seven times in eight seasons starting in 2004.

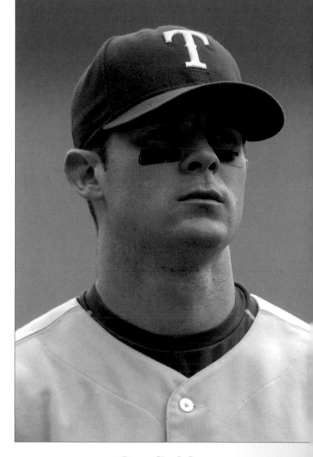

IAN KINSLER   Second Baseman

- BORN: 6/22/1982
- FIRST YEAR WITH TEAM: 2006

Baseball teams love players with power and speed. In 2009, Ian Kinsler became only the second AL second baseman to hit more than 30 homers and steal more than 30 bases in the same season. In 2011, Kinsler did it again!

JOSH HAMILTON   Outfielder

- BORN: 5/21/1981   • FIRST YEAR WITH TEAM: 2008

Josh Hamilton left baseball for three years to battle a *drug addiction*. He recovered and returned to the game. In 2008, he led the AL with 130 RBIs. In 2010, Hamilton won the league batting championship with a .359 average and was named AL MVP.

LEFT: Rafael Palmeiro   **ABOVE**: Michael Young

Finding the right manager for a team is one of the most difficult tasks in baseball. The Rangers have hired some of the brightest field leaders in the game. The same was true of the Senators before

them. During the 1960s, Gil Hodges and Ted Williams managed the club. In the 1970s and 1980s, Billy Martin, Don Zimmer, and Bobby Valentine took the job. All were respected baseball men, but none could deliver a pennant.

For most of the 1990s, Johnny Oates managed the Rangers. Oates helped Texas reach the playoffs three times from 1996 to 1999. The Rangers had great hitting under Oates, but their pitching was never quite good enough to take them to the World Series.

In 2007, the Rangers turned to Ron Washington. "Wash" was a different kind of leader. When the Rangers did well, he jumped

around the dugout like a Little Leaguer. When they made mistakes, he took it hard. Washington had been in baseball almost 40 years when he arrived in Texas. As a player, he spent more than 10 years in the **minor leagues** before getting a chance to win a job in the big leagues. After a short career, he became a coach.

All of those years that Washington had spent studying the game made him a great manager. He learned a lot about the strategy of baseball and how to get the most out of every player on his team. In 2010, Washington managed the Rangers to their first pennant. In 2011, he did what many thought was impossible when he led the team to their second AL championship in a row.

LEFT: Johnny Oates and Alex Rodriguez
ABOVE: Ron Washington

ONE GREAT DAY

When the Rangers and the New York Yankees met in the 2010 American League Championship Series, it seemed like old times for the two teams. They had faced each other in the playoffs three times in the past. Each time, New York went on to win the World Series, and the Rangers went home. After winning three of the first five games in the 2010 ALCS, Texas was one victory away from breaking its string of bad luck.

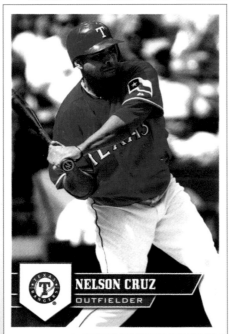

NELSON CRUZ
OUTFIELDER

The Rangers took a quick lead in the bottom of the first inning of Game 6. Elvis Andrus led off with a double and later scored on a ground ball. Meanwhile, Colby Lewis held the Yankees scoreless until the fifth inning. He threw an inside pitch to Nick Swisher that appeared to graze him and then rolled away. The umpire ruled that

LEFT: Nelson Cruz hit two homers in the 2010 ALCS.
RIGHT: Neftali Feliz closed out the final game of the series.

NEFTALI FELIZ

TEXAS RANGERS® P

the ball did not hit Swisher, and Alex Rodriguez was able to score from third base. Texas fans grew tense. Was this the play that would give the Yankees the edge they needed?

Fear turned to joy a few minutes later when the Rangers came to bat and broke the game open. Vladimir Guerrero drove in two runs with a double, and Nelson Cruz gave Texas two more with a long home run. The Rangers added another run in the seventh inning to take a 6–1 lead. Lewis pitched one more inning. Then manager Ron Washington summoned 22-year-old Neftali Feliz to the pitcher's mound. Feliz got the final three outs, including a strikeout of Rodriguez to end the game.

"The World Series is coming to Texas!" shouted Michael Young, who was in his 10th season with Texas. "These fans have waited longer than we have. I know how bad we wanted it, and they must have wanted it more."

LEGEND HAS IT

IAN KINSLER
TEXAS RANGERS®   SECOND BASE

LEGEND HAS IT that Ian Kinsler and Nelson Cruz did. Against the Tampa Bay Rays in the 2010 playoffs, Kinsler and Cruz hit three home runs apiece. The only other teammates to do that in a postseason series were Babe Ruth and Lou Gehrig, in 1928. When the 2011 season opened, Kinsler and Cruz were at it again. They each homered in the team's first three games to set a record all their own.

ABOVE: Ian Kinsler   RIGHT: Kenny Rogers

28

LEGEND HAS IT that Al Oliver did. Oliver was a hit machine for the Rangers. In a doubleheader against the Detroit Tigers in August of 1980, he found a whole new gear. In the first game, he hit a double, triple, and home run to lead the Rangers to a 9–3 win. In the second game, Oliver hit three more home runs as Texas won 12–6. After the game, Oliver was amazed to learn that he had just set a new AL record for **total bases** in one day with 21.

WHO WAS THE FIRST 'PERFECT' LEFT-HANDED PITCHER IN THE AMERICAN LEAGUE?

LEGEND HAS IT that Kenny Rogers was. Like any player, Rogers sometimes made mistakes on the field. However, on July 28, 1994, he retired all 27 batters he faced against the California Angels. It was the first perfect game ever pitched by a left-hander in AL history.

Ten years before the Rangers played their first game in Texas, a pitcher for the Washington Senators did something that no one else in team history—or baseball history—had ever done.

His name was Tom Cheney, and he threw a good fastball and an excellent curve. Cheney, however, did not always have control of his pitches. His teammates often wondered what would happen if he had total command from the start of a game to the end.

The Baltimore Orioles found out near the end of the 1962 season. On September 12, Cheney struck out 13 Orioles in nine innings. That would be a good day's work for most pitchers, but the score was tied 1–1. The Senators and Orioles would play extra innings.

LEFT: Mickey Vernon
RIGHT: Tom Cheney

Washington's manager, Mickey Vernon, asked his pitcher if he wanted to leave the game. Cheney shook his head no. "Back in those days," he said years later, "you finished what you started."

Cheney stayed in the game and kept striking out Baltimore hitters. After 15 innings, he was still on the mound. In the top of the 16th inning, Bud Zipfel hit a home run to give the Senators a 2–1 lead. Cheney already had 20 strikeouts—more than anyone in history. In the bottom of the 16th, he struck out Dick Williams to end the game. Some have come close, but no one has ever topped Cheney's 21 strikeouts in a game.

TEAM SPIRIT

Since moving to Texas, the Rangers have worked hard to keep their fans coming to the ballpark. During the 1970s and 1980s, the team brought some of baseball's biggest stars to Texas, including Fergie Jenkins, Bert Blyleven, Goose Gossage, Gaylord Perry, and Nolan Ryan. All of these players later entered the **Hall of Fame**.

In 2004, the Rangers rewarded their loyal fans with a beautiful new stadium. Almost every year after that, more than two million people attended games. In 2011, that number soared to almost three million. Like the state the team calls home, the crowd at a Rangers game includes people of all ages and many different backgrounds. Though Texans may have their differences outside the ballpark, once inside they unite and cheer for their Rangers with one big, loud voice.

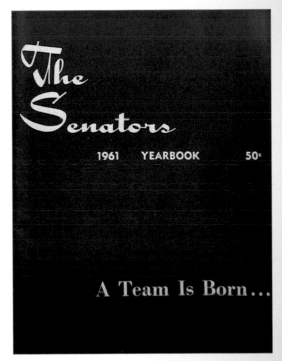

The Senators

1961   YEARBOOK   50¢

A Team Is Born...

LEFT: Texas fans rise and cheer for a "Juan Gone" home run.
ABOVE: Fans bought this yearbook in 1961, the team's first season.

TIMELINE

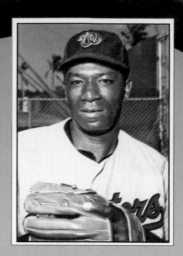

Bennie Daniels was the team's top pitcher in 1961.

1965
Relief pitcher Ron Kline leads the AL with 29 **saves**.

1972
The team moves to Texas and becomes the Rangers.

1961
The team plays its first season as the Washington Senators.

1968
Frank Howard hits 10 homers in a week.

1969
Dick Bosman leads the AL with a 2.19 **earned run average (ERA)**.

Fans bought this souvenir pennant during the team's early days in Texas.

Jim
Sundberg

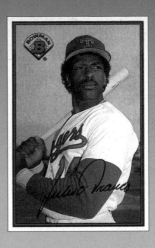

Julio
Franco

1981
Jim Sundberg wins
his sixth Gold
Glove in a row.

1996
The Rangers
reach the playoffs
for the first time.

2011
The Rangers repeat
as AL champions.

1991
Julio Franco leads
the AL with a .341
batting average.

2001
Alex Rodriguez and Rafael Palmeiro
combine to hit 99 home runs.

2010
The Rangers win
their first pennant.

Alex
Rodriguez

FUN FACTS

THE RYAN EXPRESS

In 1991, 44-year-old Nolan Ryan threw a no-hitter against the Toronto Blue Jays. It was the seventh of his career. Ryan was pitching on Fan Appreciation Night. The last batter he retired was Roberto Alomar. In Ryan's first two no-hitters, his second baseman was Sandy Alomar—Roberto's father!

SWITCH HITTER

In 2003, Michael Young played second base and had 204 hits. In 2004, he switched to shortstop and had 214 hits. It was the first time in history that an infielder changed positions and got 200 hits each year.

ABOVE: Nolan Ryan raises his leg high before delivering a pitch.

CRUZ CONTROL

In the 2011 ALCS, Nelson Cruz smashed six home runs against the Detroit Tigers. No one had ever hit more than five homers in a **postseason** series. Cruz also hit the first **walk-off grand slam** in the history of the playoffs.

LAST LAUGH

When the Rangers hired Billy Martin as their manager at the end of the 1973 season, everyone laughed after he predicted the team would be a contender and draw one million fans. In 1974, Texas finished second in the AL West and welcomed 1.2 million fans to Arlington Stadium.

THE NATURAL

In a 2006 game, Gary Matthews Jr. hit for the "natural cycle." That means he got a single, double, triple, and home run in that order. Matthews was the first Ranger to accomplish this feat.

LONG HAUL

In 1967, the Senators and Chicago White Sox played the longest night game in history. Washington won 6–5 in 22 innings. The game took six hours and 38 minutes.

"This is an awesome team to be around. Great guys. I want to be a part of that."

▶ **JOSH HAMILTON**, ON THE FAMILY FEELING IN THE TEXAS LOCKER ROOM

"You have to create a winning atmosphere. You have to trust in each other."

▶ **RON WASHINGTON**, ON WHAT IT TAKES TO BE A SUCCESSFUL MANAGER

"When I'm inside the lines, the rest of the world doesn't exist."

▶ **JUAN GONZALEZ**, ON THE FOCUS THAT HELPED HIM WIN TWO MVP AWARDS

"The way you play the game brings respect."

▶ **IAN KINSLER**, ON WHY HE ALWAYS GIVES 100 PERCENT ON THE FIELD

ABOVE: Josh Hamilton
RIGHT: Michael Young

"I play the game the way I've played since Little League."

▶ **MICHAEL YOUNG**, ON HIS PASSION FOR BASEBALL

"That's what makes this a great game...the support and the commitment that the fans give the game."

▶ **NOLAN RYAN**, ON WHAT TEXAS FANS MEAN TO THE RANGERS

"I loved Washington, loved the fans. I always said, 'The greatest fans in the world.'"

▶ **FRANK HOWARD**, ON HIS DAYS PLAYING FOR THE SENATORS

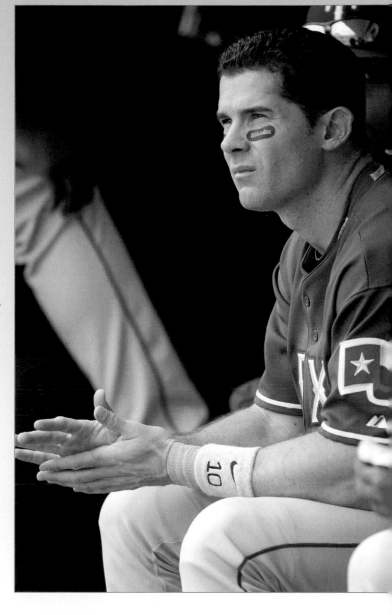

"The trouble with baseball is that it is not played the year 'round."

▶ **GAYLORD PERRY**, ON KEEPING HIMSELF BUSY AND IN SHAPE BETWEEN SEASONS

39

GREAT DEBATES

People who root for the Senators and Rangers love to compare their favorite moments, teams, and players. Some debates have been going on for years! How would you settle these classic baseball arguments?

IVAN RODRIGUEZ WAS THE TEAM'S ALL-TIME BEST CATCHER ...

... because he has the Gold Gloves to prove it. Pudge won 10 in a row with Texas from 1992 to 2001. In seven of those seasons, he was the best in the AL at throwing out base-stealers. In 1999, Rodriguez (LEFT) was named American League MVP. How do you get better than that?

PUDGE WAS GOOD, BUT NO ONE COMPARED TO JIM SUNDBERG ...

... because he was the most *agile* and athletic catcher of his time. Sundberg could not hit like Rodriguez, but he was better on defense. Sundberg played 10 years for Texas and was so impressive as a rookie that he made the All-Star team. He won six Gold Gloves as a Ranger and led AL catchers in **assists** seven times.

... because when he made solid contact, the ball launched off his bat like a rocket. Howard played for the Senators for seven seasons and spent one season with the Rangers. Every year he played in Washington, he led the team in home runs and RBIs. His nickname was the "Washington Monument." You don't get much bigger than that! In May of 1968, Howard hit 10 home runs in a week—no one has ever hit more in a seven-day period.

JOSH HAMILTON WINS THIS LONG-DISTANCE HITTING CONTEST ...

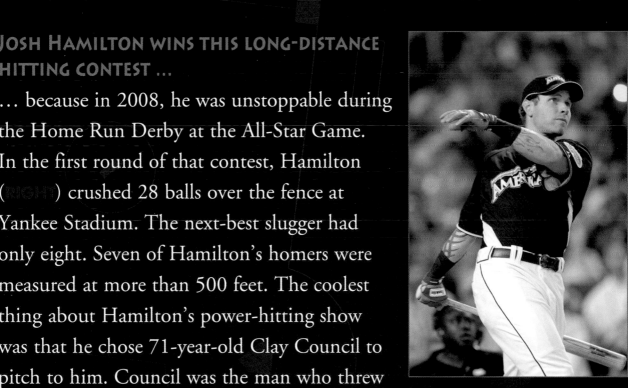

... because in 2008, he was unstoppable during the Home Run Derby at the All-Star Game. In the first round of that contest, Hamilton (RIGHT) crushed 28 balls over the fence at Yankee Stadium. The next-best slugger had only eight. Seven of Hamilton's homers were measured at more than 500 feet. The coolest thing about Hamilton's power-hitting show was that he chose 71-year-old Clay Council to pitch to him. Council was the man who threw batting practice to Hamilton when he was a boy.

Γhe great Senators and Rangers teams and players have left their marks on the record books. These are the "best of the best" ...

Ruben Sierra

MICHAEL YOUNG

Michael Young

RANGERS AWARD WINNERS

WINNER	AWARD	YEAR
Mike Hargrove	Rookie of the Year*	1974
Fergie Jenkins	Comeback Player of the Year	1974
Jeff Burroughs	Most Valuable Player	1974
Julio Franco	All-Star Game MVP	1990
Jose Guzman	Comeback Player of the Year	1991
Kevin Elster	Comeback Player of the Year	1996
Juan Gonzalez	Most Valuable Player	1996
Johnny Oates	co-Manager of the Year	1996
Juan Gonzalez	Most Valuable Player	1998
Ivan Rodriguez	Most Valuable Player	1999
Ruben Sierra	Comeback Player of the Year	2001
Alex Rodriguez	Most Valuable Player	2003
Buck Showalter	Manager of the Year	2004
Alfonso Soriano	All-Star Game MVP	2004
Michael Young	All-Star Game MVP	2006
Neftali Feliz	Rookie of the Year	2010
Josh Hamilton	Most Valuable Player	2010
Josh Hamilton	ALCS MVP	2010
Nelson Cruz	ALCS MVP	2011

The annual award given to each league's best first-year player.

RANGERS ACHIEVEMENTS

ACHIEVEMENT	YEAR
AL West Champions	1994
AL West Champions	1996
AL West Champions	1998
AL West Champions	1999
AL West Champions	2010
AL Pennant Winners	2010
AL West Champions	2011
AL Pennant Winners	2011

ABOVE: Fergie Jenkins won 25 games in 1974.
LEFT: Juan Gonzalez set a team record with 157 RBIs in 1998.

PINPOINTS

The history of a baseball team is made up of many smaller stories. These stories take place all over the map—not just in the city a team calls "home." Match the pushpins on these maps to the **TEAM FACTS**, and you will begin to see the story of the Rangers unfold!

1. Arlington, Texas—*The team has played here since 1972.*
2. San Francisco, California—*The Rangers played in the 2010 World Series here.*
3. Fort Rucker, Alabama—*Rusty Greer was born here.*
4. Savannah, Georgia—*Kenny Rogers was born here.*
5. Rocky Mount, North Carolina—*Chuck Hinton was born here.*
6. Washington, D.C.—*The team played here as the Senators from 1961 to 1971.*
7. St. Louis, Missouri—*The Rangers played in the 2011 World Series here.*
8. Portsmouth, Ohio—*Al Oliver was born here.*
9. Galesburg, Illinois—*Jim Sundberg was born here.*
10. Zeist, Netherlands—*Bert Blyleven was born here.*
11. Manati, Puerto Rico—*Ivan Rodriguez was born here.*
12. Maracay, Aragua, Venezuela—*Elvis Andrus was born here.*

Chuck Hinton

GLOSSARY

Baseball Words
Vocabulary Words

AGILE—Quick and graceful.

AL WEST—A group of American League teams that play in the western part of the country.

ALL-STAR—A player who is selected to play in baseball's annual All-Star Game.

AMERICAN LEAGUE (AL)—One of baseball's two major leagues; the AL began play in 1901.

AMERICAN LEAGUE CHAMPIONSHIP SERIES (ALCS)—The playoff series that has decided the AL pennant since 1969.

ASSISTS—Throws that lead to an out.

BULLPEN—The area where a team's relief pitchers warm up. This word also describes the group of relief pitchers in this area.

COMPLETE GAMES—Games started and finished by the same pitcher.

CONTENDERS—People who compete for a championship.

DECADE—A period of 10 years; also specific periods, such as the 1950s.

DRUG ADDICTION—Total dependence on a drug.

EARNED RUN AVERAGE (ERA)—A statistic that measures how many runs a pitcher gives up for every nine innings he pitches.

FREE AGENT—A player who is allowed to join any team that wants him.

GOLD GLOVE—The award given each year to baseball's best fielders.

HALL OF FAME—The museum in Cooperstown, New York, where baseball's greatest players are honored.

KNUCKLEBALL—A pitch thrown with no spin, which "wobbles" as it nears home plate.

LOGO—A symbol or design that represents a company or team.

MINOR LEAGUES—The many professional leagues that help develop players for the major leagues.

MOST VALUABLE PLAYER (MVP)—The award given each year to each league's top player; an MVP is also selected for the World Series and the All-Star Game.

NO-HITTERS—Games in which a team does not get a hit.

PENNANT—A league championship. The term comes from the triangular flag awarded to each season's champion, beginning in the 1870s.

PLAYOFFS—The games played after the regular season to determine which teams will advance to the World Series.

POSTSEASON—The games played after the regular season, including the playoffs and World Series.

ROOKIE—A player in his first season.

RUNS BATTED IN (RBIs)—A statistic that counts the number of runners a batter drives home.

SAVES—A statistic that counts the number of times a relief pitcher finishes off a close victory for his team.

SHUTOUTS—Games in which one team does not score a run.

TOTAL BASES—A player's total number of bases when you add up all of his hits.

WALK-OFF GRAND SLAM—A game-ending home run with the bases loaded hit in the last half of the final inning.

WORLD SERIES—The world championship series played between the American League and National League pennant winners.

EXTRA INNINGS

TEAM SPIRIT introduces a great way to stay up to date with your team! Visit our **EXTRA INNINGS** link and get connected to the latest and greatest updates. **EXTRA INNINGS** serves as a young reader's ticket to an exclusive web page—with more stories, fun facts, team records, and photos of the Rangers. Content is updated during and after each season. The **EXTRA INNINGS** feature also enables readers to send comments and letters to the author! Log onto:

www.norwoodhousepress.com/library.aspx

and click on the tab: **TEAM SPIRIT** to access **EXTRA INNINGS**.

Read all the books in the series to learn more about professional sports. For a complete listing of the baseball, basketball, football, and hockey teams in the **TEAM SPIRIT** series, visit our website at:

www.norwoodhousepress.com/library.aspx

ON THE ROAD

TEXAS RANGERS
1000 Ballpark Way
Arlington, Texas 76011
(817) 273-5222
texas.rangers.mlb.com

**NATIONAL BASEBALL
HALL OF FAME AND MUSEUM**
25 Main Street
Cooperstown, New York 13326
(888) 425-5633
www.baseballhalloffame.org

ON THE BOOKSHELF

To learn more about the sport of baseball, look for these books at your library or bookstore:

- Augustyn, Adam (editor). *The Britannica Guide to Baseball*. New York, NY: Rosen Publishing, 2011.

- Dreier, David. *Baseball: How It Works*. North Mankato, MN: Capstone Press, 2010.

- Stewart, Mark. *Ultimate 10: Baseball*. New York, NY: Gareth Stevens Publishing, 2009.

INDEX

PAGE NUMBERS IN **BOLD** REFER TO ILLUSTRATIONS.

ABOUT THE AUTHOR

MARK STEWART has written more than 50 books on baseball and over 150 sports books for kids. He grew up in New York City during the 1960s rooting for the Yankees and Mets, and was lucky enough to meet players from both teams. Mark comes from a family of writers. His grandfather was Sunday Editor of *The New York Times,* and his mother was Articles Editor of *Ladies' Home Journal* and *McCall's.* Mark has profiled hundreds of athletes over the past 25 years. He has also written several books about his native New York and New Jersey, his home today. Mark is a graduate of Duke University, with a degree in history. He lives and works in a home overlooking Sandy Hook, New Jersey. You can contact Mark through the Norwood House Press website.